Prototyping Your Inventions

By Kristin Fontichiaro and Quincy de Klerk

CHERRY LAKE
Publishing

Published in the United States of America by
Cherry Lake Publishing
Ann Arbor, Michigan
www.cherrylakepublishing.com

Series Editor: Kristin Fontichiaro
Photo Credits: Cover and pages 16 and 18, Kristin Fontichiaro;
pages 4, 6, 8, and 20, public domain via Pixabay.com; pages 10
and 12, Quincy de Klerk; page 14, Kristin Fontichiaro/Michigan
Makers.

Library of Congress Cataloging-in-Publication Data
Names: Fontichiaro, Kristin, author. | De Klerk, Quincy, author.
Title: Prototyping your inventions / by Kristin Fontichiaro and Quincy de Klerk.
Description: Ann Arbor, Michigan : Cherry Lake Publishing, [2018] | Series:
   Makers as innovators junior | Series: 21st century skills innovation library |
   Audience: Grade K to grade 3. | Includes bibliographical references and index.
Identifiers: LCCN 2017000109| ISBN 9781634726924 (lib. bdg.) | ISBN
   9781634727587 (pdf) | ISBN 9781634727259 (pbk.) | ISBN 9781634727914
   (ebook)
Subjects: LCSH: Prototypes, Engineering—Juvenile literature.
Classification: LCC TS171.8 .F66 2018 | DDC 620/.0042—dc23 LC record available at
   https://lccn.loc.gov/2017000109

Cherry Lake Publishing would like to acknowledge the work of the Partnership for
21st Century Learning. Please visit *www.p21.org* for more information.

Printed in the United States of America
Corporate Graphics

Note: Squishy Circuits® is a registered trademark of Squishy Circuits Store, LLC, and is
used with permission.

A Note to Adults: Please review the instructions for the activities in this book before allowing children to do them. Be sure to help them with any activities you do not think they can safely complete on their own.

A Note to Kids: Be sure to ask an adult for help with these activities when you need it. Always put your safety first!

Table of Contents

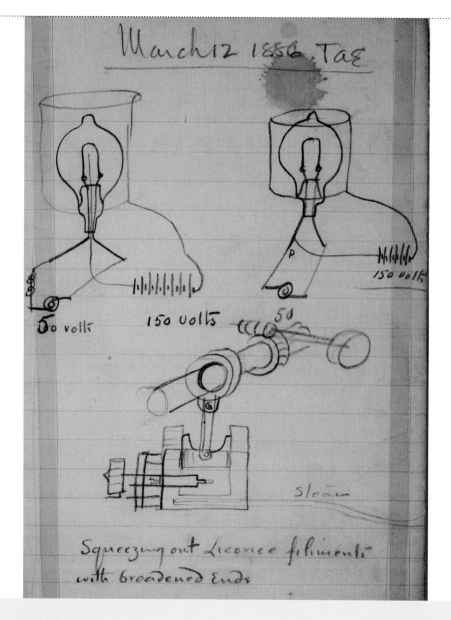

Inventor Thomas Edison made many prototypes, including this drawing. Eventually, he figured out how to make a real lightbulb!

Are You an Inventor?

Do you like solving problems? Do you like making things? Maybe you are an inventor! An inventor turns ideas into things. It takes a long time to get it just right. Along the way, inventors make many **models** of their **product**. These models are called **prototypes**. Prototypes are like sample inventions made out of simple materials like cardboard.

Wow! What a big bottle! How could he carry it more easily?

Inventing Is a Process

Inventing doesn't happen in an instant. It is a process with many steps. First, think of problems you would like to solve. These problems can give you ideas about what to make. For example, maybe you think it is hard to carry a water bottle around all day. Let's **research** and prototype a water bottle carrier!

Good Inventors Are Patient

Great ideas don't always come right away. Be patient. The prototyping process helps your ideas get better and better as you go.

Look around at the many kinds of water bottles in your school. Which features do you like? How could you carry these?

Do Research

Look up some photos of water bottles to get ideas. Which bottle features do you like? Flip lid? Screw top? Strap? Bag? Clip? What are the bottles made of? Metal? Plastic? Glass? How big are they? Make notes. Take photos. Draw pictures. When you think you have the right idea in mind, it's time to prototype.

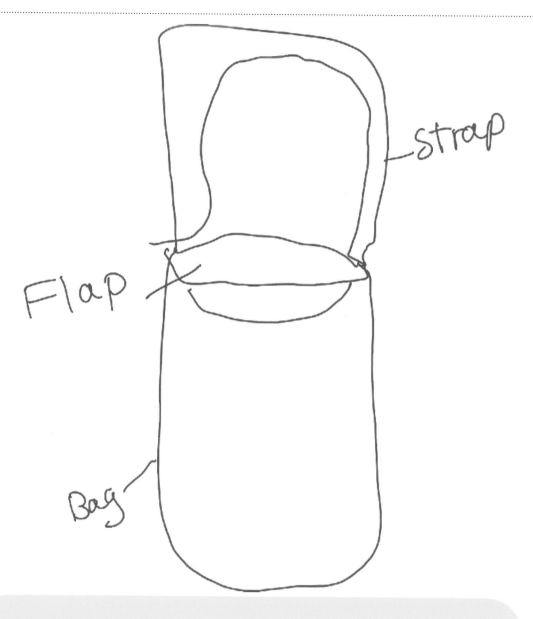

Paper prototypes show your invention with labels. Quincy's design is a bag with a strap and a flap. The bottle goes inside the bag.

Make a Paper Prototype

Decide on your favorite design. Draw it on paper. Use pencil. Draw lightly at first. This way, you can erase it if you change your mind. Label the parts. Describe what each part does. What will you make it out of? What does your product look like from the side? The top? The bottom?

Wireframing

People who design Web sites or apps sometimes call their paper prototypes **wireframes**. They draw boxes where each kind of information goes. They do not include the actual text or images—just boxes!

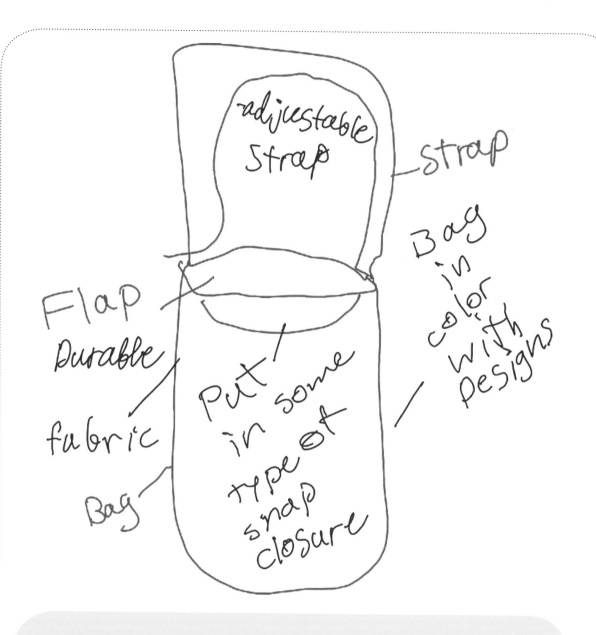

Quincy shared his paper prototype with others. Then he made notes right on the design.

Share Your Paper Prototype

Now your design is on paper. It's not just in your imagination! Show it to friends and family. Ask them what they think. Here are some good questions to ask: Do you think this is a good size? Does it look too heavy? Too big? Is this something you would use?

Good inventors collect paper, cardboard, recyclable items, and more in a "junk box." When creativity hits, they have plenty of materials ready to use.

Make a Prototype You Can Use

Use cardboard, recycled materials, fabric, or other things to build the water bottle holder you designed on paper. You might need scissors, glue, a stapler, or tape. Don't worry if it looks rough. A prototype helps people get the main idea of your invention. If it looks too perfect, you won't want to change it later!

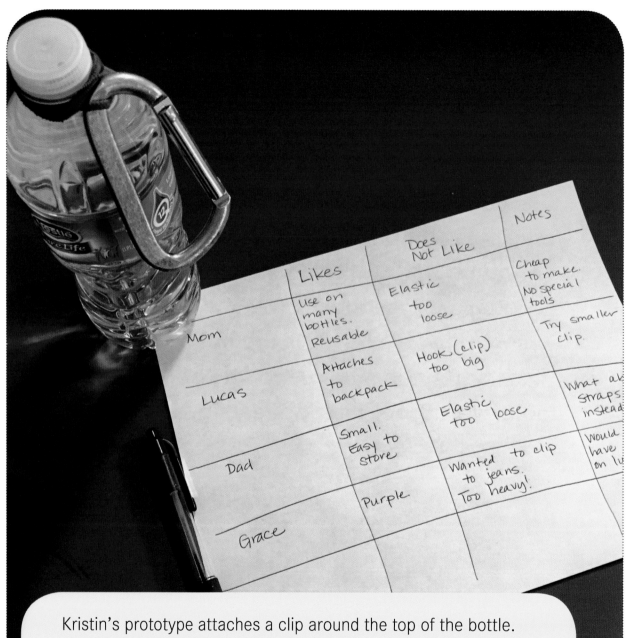

	Likes	Does Not Like	Notes
Mom	Use on many bottles. Reusable	Elastic too loose	Cheap to make. No special tools
Lucas	Attaches to backpack	Hook (clip) too big	Try smaller clip.
Dad	Small. Easy to store	Elastic too loose	What ab straps instead
Grace	Purple	Wanted to clip to jeans. Too heavy!	Would have on l

Kristin's prototype attaches a clip around the top of the bottle.
Taking notes helps you remember feedback.

Test Your Prototype

Get a water bottle. (Water is heavy, so use a full bottle.) Put it in your holder prototype. Try carrying it around. Ask friends to try it, too. They might give you **feedback** like "This is too heavy" or "This part needs to be stronger" or "This looks weird" or "This is great!"

Helpful Feedback

Try not to take feedback personally. Listen to your friends' honest ideas. This will help you make the best invention. Take notes so you remember their ideas.

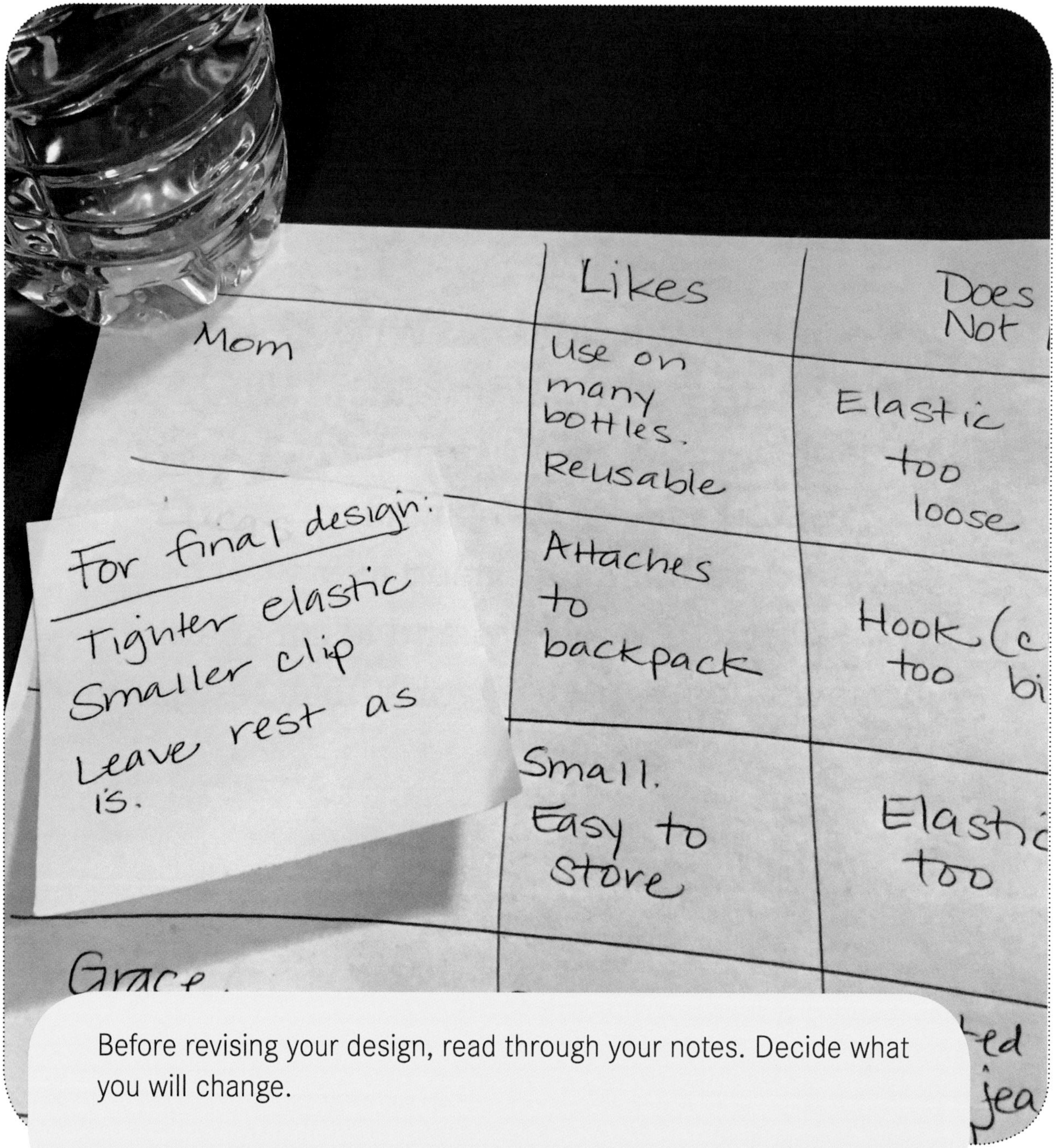

	Likes	Does Not
Mom	Use on many bottles. Reusable	Elastic too loose
	Attaches to backpack	Hook (c too bi
	Small. Easy to store	Elastic too
Grace		

Handwritten note:

For final design:
Tighter elastic
Smaller clip
Leave rest as is.

Before revising your design, read through your notes. Decide what you will change.

Revise Your Prototype

Look at the notes you took. What did people like about your invention? What didn't they like? Think about their suggestions. Decide which things need to be changed. You might need to make another paper prototype and test it again. Or maybe you are ready for a final design.

If you make your design out of fabric, you might need an adult to help you use a sewing machine to finish it.

Next Steps

Now you can make your water bottle holder for real! Find an adult who knows how to make things out of the materials you picked. Make one for yourself. Make a few for friends. Try making ones that are bigger or smaller. Thanks to prototyping, you are now an inventor of something people want and need. Congratulations!

Glossary

feedback (FEED-bak) advice from other people

models (MAH-duhlz) stand-ins for a real object

product (PRAH-dukt) the thing you make

prototypes (PROH-toh-types) rough drafts of an invention or idea

research (REE-serch) to study and learn more about something

wireframes (WYE-ur-fraymz) drawings of an app or Web page that have boxes instead of actual information

Find Out More

Books

Cook, Eric. *Prototyping*. Ann Arbor, MI: Cherry Lake Publishing, 2015.

Fontichiaro, Kristin. *Design Thinking*. Ann Arbor, MI: Cherry Lake Publishing, 2015.

Web Sites

Crazy Kids' Inventions Turned into Real Products
www.boredpanda.com/kids-inventions-turned-into-reality -inventors-project-dominic-wilcox
See cool things invented by real kids!

U.S. Patent and Trademark Office
www.uspto.gov/kids
Learn more about inventing with activities and games.

Index

About the Authors

Kristin Fontichiaro teaches and makes things at the University of Michigan School of Information. Quincy de Klerk loves technology and making things.